JOEY GOULD

The Acute Avian Heart

LILY POETRY REVIEW BOOKS

Copyright © 2019 by Joey Gould

Published by Lily Poetry Review Books
223 Winter Street
Whitman, MA 02382

https://lilypoetryreview.blog/

ISBN:978-1-7337683-4-4

All rights reserved. Published in the United States by Lily Poetry Review Books.
Library of Congress Control Number: 2019950268

Cover Design: Martha McCollough
Cover Art: Julia Moon

for Shari, Kolleen, & July

***

"Why was her body sluggish with desire?
Stark on the open field the moonlight fell,
But the oak tree's shadow was deep and black and secret as a well."
　　　　　　　　　-Edna St. Vincent Millay, "Sonnet X"

ACKNOWLEDGEMENTS:

Many thanks to those who made this book happen—

Eileen Cleary, whose guidance has made this book what I always hoped it would be, in thought, feeling, & form.

Thanks also to Martha McCollough, J.D. Scrimgeour, Kolleen Carney Hoepfner, Shari Caplan, July Westhale, Casey Roland, Julia Sparenberg, Sam Witt, Lisa Mangini, Peggi McCarthy, Jeanne Obbard, Heather Hughes, Alan Feldman, Jennifer Martelli, MP Carver, Georgia Park, Simeon Berry, LaDonna Bridges, January Gill O'Neil, Mass Poetry, The Poetry Society of New York, & everyone at Salem Writers Group.

Thanks to family & friends whom I portray here in various degrees of truth, including Penelope Gould-McCarthy, Jessica & Chris Nazca, Jennifer Demanche, Julie Oliver, Kat Suwalski, & April Wilhelm Adams. Also, the late Francis Joseph McCarthy, Sue Auger, & Colleen Harrigan.

For writing spaces: Broadmoor Audubon Sanctuary, Salem State University, & the Salem Athenaeum. Morning Garden Artists Retreat, hosted wonderfully by Jennifer & Sebastian Jean, is where the form of this book took shape & many of its pages were written. Kolleen & Fritz Hoepfner lent space wherein "Hard Turn" was first conceived. July Westhale & AC Panella hosted me as I wrote much of "when I was a man".

For becoming beloved journal homes to previous versions of my work:
The Compassion Anthology (Excerpts from "Hard Turn", 'Study: Mom on One of the Last Fine Days of Fall", "Three Doors")
Drunk Monkeys ("Poem to my Sparrow Heart", "Veery")
Five:2:One ("the most ever after")
Lily Poetry Review ("Last Meal")
Masspoetry.org ("The First Day")

& the birds.

HARUSPEX

- 3   DEVARIM
- 5   POEM TO MY SPARROW HEART
- 7   VEERY
- 8   ACUTE AVIAN HEART
- 10   THRUSHES
- 14   ON HALF MOON BEACH
- 15   THREE DOORS
- 17   NEW YEAR'S EVE

STARLING

- 21   MARATHON
- 23   [O DEAR STARLING]
- 25   [A MYTH OF WHO WOULD FEED HIM]
- 26   [THE BASS NOTES TASTE LIKE GERANIUMS]
- 29   THE MOST EVER AFTER, OR, VENUS IN THE 3RD HOUSE OF CANCER
- 31   MUSIC I HEARD WHEN I LEARNED TO TRUST
- 32   ON SUNDAY, BETWEEN CUTS

HARD TURN

- 35   LAST MEAL
- 37   HARD TURN
- 45   MIRACLE
- 47   [I WEAR THE DRESS   DESPERATE]

WHEN I WAS A MAN

- 53   THE FIRST DAY
- 54   BEING VULNERABLE, CUTTING WOOD
- 55   THE DRUM SANDING KIT
- 56   [THE DESERT STRETCHED FROM MY COLLARBONE DOWN]
- 57   [WHAT IF THE WALL WAS MY STEPFATHER'S BODY]
- 58   [AFTER A DAY OF PLASTER]

59   [SO SUE *WASN'T FEELING SO GOOD* THAT MORNING]
61   [I DON'T BLAME HIM]
63   [THE HAPPIEST I SAW FRANK]
65   [AFTER A VAN FLOODWASHED INTO THE INCONVENIENT CLIFF-EDGE]
67   [F—'S 2-YEAR-OLD NEPHEW DRIVES HIS MATCHBOX CAR]
68   PILEATED
69   EULOGY
70   STUDY: MOM ON ONE OF THE LAST FINE DAYS OF FALL
71   BROKEN & FIXED
73   ABOUT THE AUTHOR

The Acute Avian Heart

HARUSPEX

DEVARIM
"Eleh ha-devarim"—these are the words (Deut 1:1)

Like stacked rocks, be precarious
& tall—hear the high tide

at Half-Moon, louder
than yesterday. Moses:

you can be your own Aaron.
Speak to whom you're sweet on.

If she holds to you only a taut strand
of pity she still cares;

otherwise potable water
will come from the rocks

& who cares if you take the credit?
You will not be denied

the crossing of the Jordan—
you will already have reached

the Galilee. There was a song
about a man who loved Kinneret,

written by a man who loved
Kinneret. You wandered 40 years

of Aramaic desert to turn
all salts out like Philistines,

to dip your hat in & drink.

Cross out every time you've said, Maybe,

for manna *did* fall. It tastes like
genuine affection—not even love, but sweet:

a still, low lake.

POEM TO MY SPARROW HEART

You'll never bring yourself to enjoy the actual
sparrow, only its sound, the idea, its chip,
the pluck to stay when friends migrate.
Julie leaves the coast for the lakes

then stumbles home. You kiss her
cheek, look not to her eyes
but to the long expanse of sea she claimed.
Shades of ocean, countless. Tree-swallow teal,

barista-hair blue with flecks of bleach at the ends.
Also: thrushes, even through the cold,
that come around as friendships.
Another knocking at the window he knows

is yours even with the lights closed
around the house—songs of return
don't always comfort. Some sing
the boundary of a windowpane, others

use owl howls, unattainable in canopy.
You, a faint red halo half-heartedly tracking.
Hold up for him an oak leaf from your limbs,
thicker than paper but full of holes

as you pretend this is about taking a stroll.
The next day you walk in the Audubon park
to the waterline, feeling like a siren, only
no wrecks. It is sunny out, barefoot

the sand stings. Wade into singe again
as you will, as it is written
on the thousand envelopes scattered
across your bed. Are you awake?

Smell the petrichor. Rain is coming,
rain has been. After thunderstorms
you wait in your parents' bed again, listening
for the katydids to tell you: it's over.

VEERY

Excruciating reflection of the sun
on the water & you, staring
at an oblique tree after a trill—

the sea never mattered. Your friend
last night said the coast was the only
reason she could stand as she stood

under a tree smoking, & you looked
behind her at a grafted branch
braced & tied to a driftwood splint

as if it could heal
or maybe since it never will.
You aren't listening.

Listening never mattered, only
standing under a broken limb
as she talked about some boy.

Somehow you all manage to be friends
though she used to get blitzed
& kiss you. Never sober.

You love her. You love veeries.
Inchworms. Why?
The bird illuminating the tree,

the bug folding & pressing until if:
if wind conditions, if travel plans,
the weather cooperating just right.

Then the veery bolts over the sound,
unimpressive to look at, sure,
but tugging long after you lose sight.

ACUTE AVIAN HEART

Long underwater trench,
vein of delicious ore,
pickaxe unglued from haft.
The tunnel collapsed. Silly me
with no keystone, staring out
the same office window night
upon night of sunset.
I've treated my own heart like a lover
[sentient & needing wooing]
instead of squaring
my body to it, leaving room
in my atria.

              According
to the cardiac expert, acute means
proximate cause, proximate
lover. Where, god? I scream
unbelievable names of you
in a Japanese garden,
write in bars, take heart
for drinks but not home.
Waking to headaches, my cat
already at her dish. I forgot to feed her
for four years.

              I'm a liar.
I fed my own heart me. Years!
It misgrew, misliked. It flew
encaged with bent wing. It sings
the notes I'm known for: vibrato,
quavering echo. Dreaming
he'll close his eyes & listen,
he can tell me my room shape.

With a stethoscope & saw
he arrives. A pink tie, a wedding vest,
Malibu. It's Victorian but I'm Austen
so when I call, I call, *Willoughby.* Sigh
that lack of trees in the pallid foothills
hiding our seaside. When I call
I call it ours.

Maybe I should apologize
for all the iron nails. For being
a blinking highway arrow,
a lane closed. It's too late to turn
off now so we crawl toward
our rural route exits. It's too late
for it to matter—I borrowed him/her/him
like a cup of sugar. You want that
back? It's been dissolved in water.

THRUSHES

A catbird claims the maple tree
in the next yard   every morning

singing this is my tree this
is my tree

but where is *my* tree   jealously wishing
I owned   as much as I could sing

stuck with unripened pomes
hard peaches with wormholes

I am nested in a leafless gypsy moth dinner
more January than June

meanwhile   the thrushes won't shut up
at all hours   deep between boughs
how   will I find   peace

I search the bars
the dark   when I get to
The Lotus I'm already drinking
under the Christmas lights

staring   into the cloudy mirror
behind the rows of cloudy booze
a cliché   I need news

I place my hands   where
the hummingbirds live

blood marks   black wings   would you
wonder   sing of water
fowl you cannot tell apart   all
too thin to stand   you are about
to lay down   your great aunt's guidebook
forever   but then you see a blackbird
attacking a heron   too close to the nest
the desperate pecking   too small
to win   too puissant to lose

I envy
the robin's antimatter aloof eye

I don't think it remembers me

---

the car never even braked   I see
red   in her breast

in memory of Colleen

the hermit is the only thrush visible in winter
robins retreat into forest hearts

except when I needed   wings
cold   of a funeral week

conversation   I didn't know   how to speak
perched at the parlor   in a new blue

this is some   knotty
this is your   tree

not even snowing but cold   sun
sublimating   ice left on the road from

dissolving the evidence of
transmuting into a bluebird

two robins on the fence   unseasonable
& kind   their pale breasts against metal

the black   black   of their eyes
so I could look into their faint   reflective

robin   promise   blue   there would be
green   I would love   again with those

you know how birds' eyes contain all
the darkness   but are kind

in their holding the whole sadness so
you can see them   see you   seeing it

accented with a pinprick   the most pure
spectrum of unconscious hope

we now look at each other
with those eyes every time

ON HALF MOON BEACH

I will love you again
dear me   you stumbler
you swimmer   you   walking
past the boy calling your name   hey
I will write of calling   you will
right the need   to be called   of the need
of that need   someone loved your love
but not you   can I ask you
not to feel like you always have to ask
having circled yourself too long   looking
down   a pile of lanky sticks   auguring
every time you butterflied a dead breast
looking in the fridge for out-of-codes
instead of lunch   auguring sour
spoilage   circling against your own
call song   dear heart   I don't want you
to be sad   anymore   I wish
you'll be happy   you survived

listen: try to swallow
a compliment   don't take it
to the windshield   unfortunate
cicada   catch it   keep those words
in a jar on the stand   where you lay
your wallet   bring it to the beach
take off your shirt   go wading
with it   introduce it to your sadness
so they can be friends

THREE DOORS

Kindness for the wasp
was pushing open
the pollen-rich world
from exile in our house,
its head thumping against
the glass. I held
the confounding door
with fingertips in fear
of a parting sting
as it flew an S-curve
to the August sun.

How unlike the "kindness"
for the moth, September,
dew as cool as frost
on my step-father's lawn—
inside the bug wandered
the dim air as the man slept.
When it fluttered close
to the deadly vortex
of a ceiling fan, then landed
in the palm of my spread hand,
I held it out like a cross—
cradled & carried it
out the terrible door,
shaking it from my hand
regretfully, watching my own breath.
This was the same hour

of the kindness of his last breath,
past the last dose of morphine.
A man who flew
recon over agent orange forests,
then in diapers—who had

by then no strength
even to cough, who I told
goodbye as a wish, that I
could open a merciful door.

NEW YEAR'S EVE

A gasoline spill soaks the hill
of Milford Street to the drive-in
under unplowed snow
during the space-time fracture
between '05 & a snowstorm.
I lean into the rift laparoscopically,
find fibromas & a hysterectomy:
the margins are clear
but more black gut-bloom—
by the time of the scan
it has its own respiration
pressing your throat.
I thought about that
on Storrow drive—it breathed
in your neck, too. then
on Soldier's Field road,
oil fields: the Ponca refinery fires
overtake me in the passing lane—
How the fire in the throat
of a machine—April said,
Always lit. 500 fragments later
the margins are clear
the margins are clear
the six-month scan
mere excuse to skip work,
the finish of a wormhole
half, now, across the galaxy
from that sadness
from the gas gash
at the drive-in closing
the road between home
& the hospital. You loll.
Telling Kat last night
I counted all the pills
in the empty bottles
as if medicine existed.
Blood soaking through

bandages, petroleum
poured underneath:
that snow-coat over
malignancies & trees.
In two weeks,
surprising yourself,
you find you would like to survive.

STARLING

MARATHON
for Jessica & Chris

Twenty-six-point-two miles later, you:
breathing in unison, finally cooling from
exertion, desert heat of sojourn. He runs
beside, she flanks his heart. As if always
were an eye color, the blue Always you know
in your bones. Beloved, it is. A forever who

pulls corks & pours for both mouths, who
waits at the terminal at the end of ache. You
spent all those hours driving airport runs, know
the premature shares of sun, each from
each—the tulip hues, the lilac clouds always
moving east. Then, on your feet: fun runs

for the sake of aimlessness. Midnight runs
bending through dark forest with beams. Friends who
burst into a twist of leaves. Other cars pass, always
the bassline blare. Near misses. A spill. You
waited for a Samaritan with your coat pulled to.
Whirring by every pedestrian comes to know:

sidewalk trash, cracks. Then, out of the night, mirth—know
it will be. The boy from the concert will run
at her behest from Buffalo,
meet the blooming tulip horizon who
slips onto her foot a glass fractal. You
coexist with witches easily, always

reenact magic. Cobblestone footsteps always
sound haunting, October or no. You know
how to get there on foot, co-carry the torch around corners, you
share shoulders. Now the relay team runs
newly cured asphalt every dusk. Stable earth, a partner who
will apologize, or laugh & clean a carpet. Love with

dinner boiling, scenting kindness in time. Love with
the miles behind & accomplished—always
more to go but the uphill heartbreak done for two who
pace each other's breaths. The very muscles know
musical measures, length of stride, years of training runs
& trials—qualifying times plied, you

always know
who runs
with you.

[O DEAR STARLING]

                    let's build
a nest   from angery reacts
the dead   used envelopes
ripped   scavenger   heart
I will   give you my next *yes*
my upcycle   with nicks
wet feathers   I've enough
antibodies   smoke in the distance
we're both late   chasmed
bridges snapping to behind
macrophage   trail   I left
DNA there   & there   my spleen
on the backs   of envelopes
you flew   to this tree
with the forest flaming below

---

tiny drops
of rain   turn mill pond   into a quilt
of discs   holographic tapestry
who knew   that rain floats?

when the speckled chick   falls
down the chimney   who opens
the flue   holds   the little bird
to the door   in palms   soot black
or actual   the wing dots
walk the future songbird   out the door
into spring day   get the ladder   ready

[A MYTH OF WHO WOULD FEED HIM]

from her hand   his transmuting
feathers   unable to cool
there he hopped   around the meadowland
unable to unstartle   how he turned
like that   into wings

---

somewhere to rest   someone
firm enough for a nest   can't
always be in the sky   can't use
clouds   please need   to roost
to sleep perpendicular   parallel
is the L   uppercase love   constant
can turn into triangle   right
angle   o eagles need cliffs need
rock   the glitterer with white
with sepia with bark   please
sleek needs a place to preen
& fluff its stupid feathers
underneath mottles   finally
unhinge my locked gate

[THE BASS NOTES TASTE LIKE GERANIUMS]

stuck in my teeth like leaves around damp
athenaeum garden   who cares about the beaks
about the red angery green-obsessed
economics majors   when the sky
goes on slathering itself across   as
we seek a rhododendron tall enough
to stand under to flirt under the next day

to weave sticks to cook for   I felt her
stomach that morning   such delicate
all you could see was little chunks of sky
the chickadee slathered her black cap
across a beard   I heard blue bells
the rhododendron   heard not the ocean
but blue ceiling pieces strung to the chord
of whatever long vein could weave
into medical diagramming   a blue cage

holding the frets   intoning low register
into amphitheater bushes   sliced sky
in my diaphragm   jumped into the sea
of red where the waves took shells
threw them laughing into a cliff

I know what it sounds like
a dream trope   the myth of her
overlarge camphor tree   getting cut
then etched

it cannot   tell
a flame   from reflection
poor flame   moth   kissing
a mirror   so it feels its own
heat   reflected   warms itself
against metal   or whatever
the doors are made of   kisses
its hope   full on   with tongue
feels   its own powerful   heart
knows   how delicious
it tastes

THE MOST EVER AFTER, OR, VENUS IN THE 3RD HOUSE OF CANCER

acidic light   in the sky
blue-star destroyer of small-flower
wishes   yellow   yellow horizon

Lucifer Morningstar   loved once
west of the sun

the smitten asked   would it
ever support life?   is there a satellite?

no

who is smitten neglects science
chemical composition
of the beloved
astronomical distance

[the poet inaudibly says
something about time]

& wormholes   the cracked
windows after dark   the time vapors
rose from our faces   delirious
beautiful   but the pipe cached
after some months' orbit

forever locked in left-handed
spin   will never eclipse
its own fire

the closest body   but never moon

[something about time]

lament the   extremely sky
the exceeding amber   outer

atmosphere   looks so soft   even
when landing into acid

will dissolve the beloved
in seconds

& yellow   over any stretch
of time   is never blue

MUSIC I HEARD WHEN I LEARNED TO TRUST

percussion   hammer strike
& the whirr of the Dewalt   thump
against drywall & the click
of the clutch   the drill set
to lowest torque   then   gentler
sounds   a rapping like a knock
on a door when we tap in
a stair-tread while the drywall mud
dries   I run my hand on the wall
touch smoothness from rough
after we've solved the cracks
between panels   we know
to measure twice   cut once
check the number before sending
the call   I steady a 2 x 4 as you tear it
with a screeching sound   like a hawk
piercing the silence of a sky   we trust
each other to rip wood without words
box cutters sheathed   now we paint
to slake the harshness of sheetrock
screws fusing wall to form   sown in sweat
dripping into sawdust

ON SUNDAY, BETWEEN CUTS

Tim, grey hair just touching
the gold beer can near his nose,
said, Money trees would be useless
in the winter, & he rocked back
in a dust of pressure-treated shavings.

Jenn edged herself along
the naked joists of her future
deck, laughed, & said,
The tree of life would make a
great wedding gift.

Hodge, kissing her to attention,
mentioned the wedding night,
was duly slapped, & my hand
wandered off the chop-saw
as a gesture of peace—

I said, My tree would be
apologies, & Tim said,
You can build with that.

HARD TURN

LAST MEAL

I sliced & my friend
considered homelessness.
It was too much on my summer

pay. I gave him two days—
my studio had no doors
& I was used to being

alone. It was a dark
red marbled delight,
New York strip, splayed

& ready to sear. Also,
my father was near-
ly dead & for sure

I needed to grieve,
could I be a father
to anyone else?

On my couch I don't know
if he cried. I was chopping
carrots into jagged coins

& he laughingly named it
his Last Supper. I am no Father,
& he, no Son.

The merlot from my father's
last business deal? I dripped
it into the pan at the end.

He turned into script
resembling Arabic:
beautiful lines & dots

I can't read. I mean
my steak-savoring friend.
I searched for him

on Facebook so I should know.
Maybe he never ate again,
went two dimensional

or gave up on social
media. I applaud that
from five exits down

the turnpike, somewhere
I don't have to try
to cook him any food.

I am no father & watching him
drive away that night
I felt too much like one

to see him again.

HARD TURN

who comes through your walls   your men's
clothing   his hook   comes   snags
tide is a riptide   you are a man
this hook is what men do to
x   you might as well
enjoy it
shh

I have been in men's clothing   I am
sheepish   have been   I hope not
the wolf   came versed in stealing

often boys call the parallelogram
square   not understanding the lack
of right   angle   not understanding
there is a bend or
worse   bending it themselves
o they are merely   boys will be wolves
do not touch the injured dove
with your   bare

teeth   could see the coaxial cable
behind your smile   but still
bent & bent   again

can you imagine   I was a man?
I disrobe the snow to sun & mourning
doves   shed the insolent news
for trees   disrobe   I mean pull down
pull boys   pull hearts   & hem
pull myself over my shoulders like a tight
top   my belt laid off thudding
to the floor   step clean
draw shades from my room

o mama   says go outside kid
rockslide climb to the Hollywood sign
higher   on a slide rule
but really a tailor's tape measuring
glamorous   chrysalis

is love so difficult?   duh
but you phrased it as a question
every atom difficult   each love
the student kind the love kind the drinks
slinking out of the woods kind the shake
hands after five tide kind   the tide tide
the wide eye look   sunset rock slide kind
the vibrating state of   solid matter
tremors less but no one tremors none
when I touch   your positive charge
kinda hurts   o dear difficult kind
I love our disparate electricities

what this has to do with the belt:
heaviness weighed against a dress
flats against boots   choose flapper tassels
float to seven glitter directions
& the dress feels sheer   two flowers
disrobing the thud belt   layers   suits

like fingers   I have been a fist
a man now mockingbird on palm
no warning calls   the alarm dove
flickers   calms   resumes coo from the next tree

o birds' fluidity   & branch
height   projecting songs to Burbank
over the water tower   loud
with skinny wings   reach the branch
apple the apple   tassel leaves   no
belt   wind under hems   broach in hair
catbird branch   I have been a gap
now filled with bright   magnolias
was pale when skinned then
climbed   put my body through
the tree the slosh spill sun corona
soon   it means   you need shoes

shoes open toed   announce   shed
the snow   bejeweled   o kindled
with fur   there should be fire
on an arcing dune   a boy   crystal
seaside diamonds   a throng
of souls with valence when everyone
says *yes*   & never happier
to need shoes

brush   {the snow body
footprints   a belt of ice}   away
may I present the catbird & sun?
ready my doors for light
fill any gaps with wood
& lip   open shutters
the overlooking elm jealous
limbs everywhere   no fist
except fingers for the atoms

will you let you?
don't ask like it's a question

MIRACLE

goes down on that skating boy
who sliced eights   infinities
of solution   congruency proof
be the shaft-hand   heel-curved stick
in my mouth   swelling melting tide
like boys can only know how
girls can only smoke their eyes
not just vitreous but aqueous I hear
harmonies under your heave
after shift   glove it down   hold
the five-hole   butterfly in the crease
figure eight maker who would float away
escapes helium   needs anchor   keeps
skates on the ice   one knock on
the prospect was he wouldn't
fight in the corners   pulls
a tight turn on everybody with
his gun   rifles it in   his own
net   in the passenger seat

if you let me dress you
in rainbows   skates parallel
you sculpture   teenage star
exploding   slept in the passenger
seat   we're all in some passenger
seat   you are what you never
mouthed   planted   prayed
no mouth-guard muscle fists
I spill myself too in the passenger
seat   now please   chrysanthemum veins
I hold   please last the night   hold
enough blood in your moon   long
as we drive   headlights pointing
always point   at the trees
if you don't sleep you can
do human things   trip
on the carpet   wake up
your wife in the middle of the
creaking night   pause
in the hallway   not tell her
but see my three birds

[I WEAR THE DRESS   DESPERATE]

how many fingers   two
eyes   sunglasses   fogged
who doesn't want a nest?
I brought you two dumb twigs
everything I give you burns
successfully   didn't offer
my burning   o dove climb
to me   I wear my favorite
sadness   insensible
shoes   the sun failing
I do not know how
to get back down

uncatchable dove   there are many
types of life-list though I can't bear
them all in mind   & who are we?
always running to the next dune
the shadows form people & their waves
come in dark   choked   shade is
the best place on the beach   no
running down the crashing line   no
that sea-bird boulder so far out
I'd never make it back   no
the outer neck of the park & our quiet
lasts a half-hour   not touching
our phones   a détente   yes
past the incandescent bushes
an aluminum baseball bat chimes
the fathers cheering

tide brought you sleek rocks
during the night   pebbles from a giant
overzealous crow & who
loves a crow but beyond the stones
calligraphy burgundy seaweed
which may be unseemly but you gaze
down from an overbearing cliff
at the outskirts of the beach—
moon's blood coming in   high
o what now rides this tide?
Let it bring whatever it may carry,
with salt to polish wounds.
I am ready for some form
of punctuation; I will love
you. Yes, friend. In whatever tide.

WHEN I WAS A MAN

THE FIRST DAY

We knocked mom's house down
to studs. Opaque air
settled as I got
to know this man I had known
only as a handshake.
As he cut the power
I brushed walnut stain
into a newel post's grooves
& looked down at him
wiring a light switch,
spooling out wire that yellow
color of construction,
clipping, the little snip sound
of the wire cutters—

then I loved him

bent into the effort
of twisting metal
& making light.
He disappeared
into the basement
& snapped on the panel switch.
Let there be light.
I must've looked
like a confused dog, staring
tilted-head at him:
how focused,
precise,
intricate
the wiring is.

BEING VULNERABLE, CUTTING WOOD

Arsenic   copper   no
facemask   cigarettes flare
I drive & floppy
deck boards wobble
out the back of Jenn's truck
asbestos   big fucking
facemask & wet/dry vac
I drive a toe-nailed screw
drive six-hundred & sixteen
stainless steel 4-inch nails
a radiator fell
& Jenn's foot got smashed
but we keep working
even when Tim's mom dies
we pour concrete & drink

who asked the wood before
poisoning it copper
green, slicing it to strips?
part of the project
it dies   so I can plunge
the chop-saw through & tree
becomes a frame for walls
we'll line with pictures   us
laughing though slumped from
hurting ourselves   & pain
is a tool   properly used

THE DRUM SANDING KIT

tighten   the screw
a small squeeze
against the rubber tube
holds the sanding strip
fast   force down
causing expansion out
causing a tight hold

the correct
amount of friction
strengthens the bond
for all the pressure

without a firm hold
it may slip in the middle
of sanding a flat line
& wreck everything

[THE DESERT STRETCHED FROM MY COLLARBONE DOWN]

to my navel   B— climbed
on my ribs to see the stars because there was no town
there not even a base camp   his lone nightlight
like a tourist he threw water bottles around the rocks
my soil dry & all his water ran off the side of the bed

showers twice a day to get the plaster off
the pry bar black in the midst of all my clenched
fingers before my right index became a riverbed
after long after my left ring refracted

the light I demoed   wired by a snipped extension cord
which I moved again   again into positions at night
it could have burned the house down
could have killed us all

Frank could smoke a whole cigarette in five drags
walking from Dynasty to the Tahoe
after medium-rare burgers

he wanted to write poems

[WHAT IF THE WALL WAS MY STEPFATHER'S BODY]

old wainscoting like shake your head
fake wood   over horsehair & shabby lath

watch two men breathing into their masks
ceaseless debris   contractor bags full of dust

B— said it looked like I'd been to war
so I never let him see me unshowered
sometimes I couldn't lift
the swelling away from my knees
& I would forget the key code
or his dog's name

Frank kept asking if there was a girl
in my life

[AFTER A DAY OF PLASTER]

don't forget to moisturize or wear goggles
or listen or recheck the measurement
or breathe or
or tell her where you're going

We were in college so it happened in movie theatres & cars
it happened in my childhood
home that we swung & swung at
it happened in such a high flood the crops failed
the pumps failed & we carried pails
every time we left the house
we checked the notches at the levee
& shook our heads

[SO SUE WASN'T FEELING SO GOOD THAT MORNING]

& she was chopping the ice into her little bins & setting the rows of sawn filets

while I uncovered & flipped the banana boxes pyramid stacked & still green & heard her fall on her ass

& she said *I need to leave* so I carried her through the swinging doors past the soy bullshit down the green tile of the produce aisle & the lettuce was dripping crisp & I carried her past the misting kale

up past the soda football display through the skinny out doors & tossed her lengthwise into her truck where she said she'd be good &

that was it

I stacked the plastic on the white on the blue pallets & wheeled them out where they'd go back to the warehouse & that's the last time I heard her voice

---

the day before   Sue had dropped her pants in the compactor area when Bobby said something fresh

& that's how Bobby chose to remember it

[I DON'T BLAME HIM]

for taking off the ring
in the library then
S— called
& he had to think of something to say

---

the underwater valley oozed
& I took S— to *Lookout Rock*

& the bridge to the doctor's office was under,
most of the fields had ducks coasting across
their bellies & she took off her shirt
in the face of devastation
& there we were in the gap of a forest
in the center of the floodplain

the rain was so puissant & I never used the shuttle
I got so soaked that when I got to class the prof took one look at
me & pointed back out the door—
why are men?
they could act forgivable for one flicker of the tv cycle

I'll be a bird
So that's how I became a life-long Audubon member & sometimes
the explanation does ruin the magic but

that night I fed my cat a mountain of food   I went to see H—

I was helping her study I was only going to chat with him I was
having dinner she made the first move he seduced me he bought
me a drink I couldn't drive home like that she was a terrific poet so
why not she was the second in the room she had a great accent it
was a strange time for me

I always needed an excuse

[THE HAPPIEST I SAW FRANK]

was after he knew he would die
soon he said between 9 & 90 days

the day I marked up his few
poems & they were about my mother & sweet

prayers from the mountains he climbed
the apple-selling days & he thought she

was worth more than his mountains & all the apples

recently come from the northwest desert to a floodplain
a place lush enough & the birds roosted

the cat curled into the outside angle of his knees
moved into his every turn in sleep

the readjusting dark when the beloved got up
to pee or the cat clawed where his beard scraggled

its edge thin   no love like his soft-clawn neck
& cat-kneaded pierce-points to his chest

he could hear the stream flex in the cross-yard
& each in its own pursuit of sleep: man giving his bare

chest to the claw, claw giving itself to a familiar body
& the stream yawning at them from the treeline

---

tell me honest that's never been you with kneading talon
& your beloved struggling to find it cute

how far you'd go down his throat for that threshold
how exactly you can gauge an edge

[AFTER A VAN FLOODWASHED INTO THE INCONVENIENT CLIFF-EDGE]

of a ravine they welded bars through its burnt husk

so tourists rappel—in the windshield   out its back doors

to keep welding ribs in is one way
we proceed through carcasses
washed into valleys

directions: past the dead through the skull then down to the desert floor

---

N— started shaking she chose me beside her for the 40-foot rock face
one hand on her back one on the rope & I could talk all day how hard it hurt
instead of remembering how scared she was falling backward
headfirst through its skull to the desert floor where we made a fire to brew delicious tea
as if she hadn't just punched her own flaming ghost in the face
& I remarked how it was my hand between her & demise

I came a Pisces born in a snowstorm when I walked to G--'s house
after four inches had fallen
& I hated G— but he came

on my face

so I couldn't have hated him that much

N— had a gun on her back as I walked behind her up the hill &
past the ibex

leaving her panic in the desert where it belonged & soon we'd be in
Eilat & its casinos
its street-vendor trinkets & the blue necklace
I didn't know I loved until it was around my neck

but we hadn't gotten to the sea yet & it felt arduous & stupid be-
cause some of us had guns where we could put hands
which would you want on your bare spine? of course

also the medic was insane & when he offered me weed in the hostel
I didn't know how to tell him no
then he knew I didn't know how to tell him no

he had a gun
& there was water there
we were both parched

[F—'S 2-YEAR-OLD NEPHEW DRIVES HIS MATCHBOX CAR]

on the deck railing
& I wondered how Frank would've looked at me
I only knew him grown   almost peers
mostly holding weapons

I wish I had turned & seen him watching me tearing into the
dining room wall
did he look? were his glasses fogged? was his trigger finger barking
at him?
did he see my shirtless shoulders

like I once saw G—'s kneeling over a lithograph machine
& I wanted him to paint me a new room
I wanted him to nail pictures to me
I could've had ten hands on him

I made a house in that tanned body
or what I touched   every time I drank
& felt light wind pick up my sun-bleached hair

coming home darker & with strange silver gifts
& were my ribs bigger?   & were the rooms smaller
in the houses I came back to   the people

were rooms I slept in   all my fathers unaware
I greeted dad like prodigal   ready for a feast
but our tents are us & not where we sleep

PILEATED

ruddy pattern   skirt   patchwork
crisp lines   your lines   underlined
remember   half a dragon age
a human ago   I don't
remember   said   didn't say
but little loops into my notebook
flourishes   editorial
few words worthy   o your waves
were another language class
in a pinup   on the palm   marked
time   I drank across the bar from
who turned into a pattern   it makes
sense but when?   when I recall
plaid   this instead you
the skirt version   of Joseph's
coat   now if only   please
7 years   of plenty   I'm ready
to admit   love   in this age
of avian flu   wire perches
like skirt lines   I wore my dreams
you wore that skirt   whitecaps
at your kneecaps   rush over the sound

EULOGY

long after   light from the nova
touched his   celestial body
sharply beautiful against black
canvas   I hold sandpaper he used
to smooth a plane wing that lifted
the Curtiss Jenny   into the sky

STUDY: MOM ON ONE OF THE LAST FINE DAYS OF FALL

Mom looks small in the yard
with her tall thin rake sweeping
up the trees as they crumple
& I help her bag the stricken
giants' guts. The day is chill—
as crisp as a glass of wine, nearly
bitter like anything savory—
so we're locking up the world
for winter & then
there are boxes, always
more boxes of his stuff
to give or file or toss,
but at least she can be outside
that mess for a while longer,
trading the extinguished light
for the waning reds & oranges
of fall. Raking as a tribute—
collecting deaths, making them
seem containable.

BROKEN & FIXED

Lord of the
almost disaster
he cut through
the cord of the jigsaw
with the jigsaw   then
30 minutes later I heard
the hum of it again
he had fixed
the damn thing

I talk to him
when anything breaks
what he touched works
even the old clock
that had stopped still
still chimes on time

so he is not dead
though today I killed
his jigsaw for good
shaping risers out of birch
making new steps to the hot tub
he built a 12 x 14 deck to hold

when mom & I go up
then plop down into the heat
in winter
from frozen to warmth
we find ourselves
immersed in him
as the steam seeps up
but falls back down
as snow

ABOUT THE AUTHOR

Jessica Lynne Furtado // jj lynne photography

Joey Gould is a writing tutor from a town originally established as a utopian society. Since 2011, they helped orchestrate each iteration the Massachusetts Poetry Festival in Salem, MA. In addition, they have written articles for Masspoetry.org & traverse MA as a workshop leader for Student Day of Poetry events in schools. They volunteer for The New York City Poetry Festival & perform as Izzie Hexxam in The Poetry Society of New York's Poetry Brothel. Always willing to entertain, they have joined a poetry circus, improv comedy/poetry events, & a poems-to-order art gallery event. They curated a special issue section of *Soundings East* as a returning fellowship alum of & generative workshop leader for The Salem State University Summer Poetry Seminar. A poetry editor in their own right (formerly of *Golden Walkman* & presently at *Drunk Monkeys*) their poetry can be found in issues of *Five:2:One*, *Lily Poetry Review*, *District Lit*, *Memoir Mixtapes*, & *The Compassion Anthology*, amongst others. They have been a Mass Audubon member since 2008.

www.ingramcontent.com/pod-product-compliance
Lightning Source LLC
Chambersburg PA
CBHW060503080526
44584CB00015B/1533